Productivity and Prices

Productivity and Prices

The Consequences of Industrial Concentration

Steven Lustgarten

American Enterprise Institute for Public Policy Research
Washington and London

Steven Lustgarten is a professor of economics and finance and a research associate at the Center for the Study of Business and Government, Baruch College, City University of New York.

338.8
L 972 p

Library of Congress Cataloging in Publication Data

Lustgarten, Steven.
    Productivity and prices.

    (AEI studies ; 392)
    Includes bibliographical references.
    1. Industrial concentration–United States.
2. Industrial productivity–United States. 3. Price
policy–United States. 4. United States – Manufactures.
I. Title. II. Series.
HD2785.L87   1984   338.8'0973   83–17133

ISBN 0–8447–3536–1

AEI Studies 392

Printed in the United States of America

Contents

LIST OF FIGURES

Foreword

The declining rate of productivity growth experienced by the United States and many other industrial countries in the past fifteen years has had a significant impact on the recent economic performance of these countries. It has affected their economic growth, inflation, and overall economic competitiveness. Yet the origins and causes of this decline are not particularly well known and remain a puzzle to many experts in the field.

Given this gap in our knowledge, AEI decided two years ago to embark on a multiyear project focusing on the causes and implications of the decline in productivity growth. The objective was to analyze the contributing factors to this decline and to assess the likely effects of existing or proposed policies upon the functioning of certain sectors of the economy and upon costs, prices, and employment.

In this spirit and as part of the ongoing program of AEI, Professor Lustgarten in this volume analyzes recent trends in industrial concentration and their implications for prices and productivity. Lustgarten attempts to explain the evolution of industrial hierarchies and structures and its effect on current or possible antitrust regulation and public-policy choice.

His analysis leads to the observation that economic development and technological evolution have had a similar pattern in many industrialized countries: Atomistic market structures (many small firms) have been replaced by oligopolistic structures (a few large firms). The change has occurred either through mergers and acquisitions, through internal expansion of some of the more successful firms, or through bankruptcy of the less successful firms.

Although the efficiencies of mass production techniques, economies of scale, are well recognized economically, government opposition to the growth of large-sized firms in the United States, evidenced by the growth of antitrust policies, has been periodically observed. Those who wish to break up large firms with significant market shares in certain industries base their argument on what is called a monopoly theory of concentration. This theory argues that strong oligopolistic firms basically function like a monopoly and thus dampen economic competition, pursue predatory pricing policies to drive competing firms out of the market, and resort to excessive advertising campaigns in order to create barriers to the entry of new firms. In contrast to this argument is the efficiency theory, which holds that concentration arises out of a competitive process in which the less efficient firms are replaced by cost-saving, resource-saving, efficient firms. If this latter argument is correct, then government policies designed to restructure concentrated industries will lead to inefficient production and higher prices for consumers.

Lustgarten's study analyzes changes in productivity and price levels in U.S. industries that have accompanied changes in seller concentration over the last quarter century. His findings show that concentration has not led to poor productivity performance or necessarily to higher prices. His data refute the monopoly theory in favor of the efficiency theory and suggest that legislation to retard concentration of major manufacturing industries could actually have unfavorable effects on consumer welfare.

The views expressed in the study are, of course, solely those of the author and should not be ascribed to the trustees, officers, or other associates of the American Enterprise Institute.

William J. Baroody, Jr.
President
American Enterprise Institute

1
Introduction

Changes in industry structure among industrialized countries have followed a similar pattern. Industries initially composed of many firms underwent a transformation whereby a few large companies came to account for the majority of sales. Mergers and acquisitions, internal expansions of the more successful firms, and voluntary liquidations or bankruptcies of the less successful firms produced this change.

The fact that the same industries have become concentrated in most modern national economies suggests that basic economic forces rather than chance occurrence are behind such changes.[1] Technological progress, for example, has decreased the cost of transportation, enabling efficient firms to market their output to an enlarged territory. The most frequently cited determinants of industrial structure, however, are the technological improvements that underlie economies of scale in production. The use of highly specialized labor and equipment on assembly lines, and of continuous refining and processing, and other methods of mass production are among the principal means of achieving efficiency. But to employ these means most efficiently, firms must typically achieve a large size and produce a very large volume of goods. In many industries, the volume required for a firm to use all these specialized factors and to substitute continuous production methods for batch processing means that only a few firms can exist.

Of course, movement from an atomistic to a concentrated industry structure is not the only pattern found. Some industries, such as aluminum, computers, electric lamps, and man-made fibers, that are now oligopolistic were highly concentrated from their inception. Other industries began concentrated and became atomistic.[2] The cotton textile industry in the United States, for example, had a four-firm concentration ratio of 90 percent in 1800, but the ratio had dropped to 8

This study was carried out with the help of Jack Farkas, who provided assistance in assembling the data base. The author thanks Yale Brozen for his extensive comments on earlier drafts and his numerous suggestions for incorporating additional material. Responsibility for any errors or omissions is entirely the author's. Financial assistance for the project was provided by the General Electric Foundation.

1

TABLE 1

Manufacturing Value Added, by Four-Firm Concentration, 1972

Four-Firm Concentration Ratio	Percentage Share of Value Added
0–0.09	5.29
0.10–0.19	17.67
0.20–0.29	18.69
0.30–0.39	14.87
0.40–0.49	13.10
0.50–0.59	7.49
0.60–0.69	9.88
0.70–0.79	4.10
0.80–0.89	1.44
0.90–1.00[a]	7.47
Total	100.00
Weighted average concentration	40.20

a. For the telephone and telegraph apparatus industry, the 1970 figure of 0.94 was used. The Census Bureau could not disclose the data for 1972.
SOURCE: U.S. Department of Commerce, Bureau of the Census, Census of Manufacturers, 1972, *Concentration Ratios in Manufacturing*, MC76(SR)-2, table 5.

percent by 1840. The structure of the U.S. meat-packing industry was initially atomistic, became concentrated, then became deconcentrated. The ready-to-eat cereals industry started out concentrated, became deconcentrated, then became reconcentrated.

Most of the national output in the United States is produced in industries where the largest firms account for only a small fraction of the national market. In manufacturing, only 30 percent of the value added is produced in industries where the four largest sellers account for more than 50 percent of industry sales nationally (see table 1). In other sectors of the economy, such as agriculture, construction, mining, and retail trade, average concentration is even lower than that in manufacturing. Communications—network radio and television, telephone, and the postal service—subcategories of transportation such as bus and railroad passenger service, and government are the major exceptions. In this study the manufacturing sector of the United States will be analyzed in an attempt to determine whether consumers were made better off or worse off when industries became more concentrated.

Criticism of Concentration

Although the efficiencies of large-scale production are well recognized, opposition to the growth of large firms in the United States has appeared periodically in various forms. An early instance was the Pujo Committee investigation of 1913 which looked at the concentration of control over wealth by the financial community.[3] In 1938–1941, the Temporary National Economic Committee investigated the extent and the effects of high seller concentration in the industrial sector. It concluded that a reorganization of the economy was necessary.[4] More recently, in 1968, a Task Force on Antitrust Policy, appointed by President Lyndon Johnson, recommended a "Concentrated Industries Act" that would direct the attorney general to examine all concentrated or oligopolistic industries—there defined as those in which the four largest firms sell 70 percent or more of the domestic output of the industry—and bring legal proceedings against firms with a market share of 15 percent or more.[5] In 1972 and again in 1975, an industrial reorganization bill was introduced in the U.S. Senate. Its aim was to dissolve the largest firms in any industry in which the four largest sellers produced 50 percent or more of domestic output.[6] Under the bill, the reorganization of certain industrial sectors was to take priority. These included chemicals and drugs, electrical machinery, energy, iron and steel, motor vehicles, electronic computing, and nonferrous metals.

Those who wish to deconcentrate major industries base their arguments on what can be called the shared-monopoly, or collusion, theory of concentration. According to that theory, in any industry in which sellers are few, the sellers will recognize their interdependence and collude—either tacitly or overtly—to restrict output so as to achieve a monopoly price.[7] Existing levels of concentration are the result of mergers that were aimed at the achievement of monopoly power, predatory pricing policies that drove out competitive firms, and excessive advertising, which blocked other firms from entering the industry.[8] High prices persist in concentrated industries, according to this theory, because the threats of predatory pricing and advertising restrict entry.

These arguments contrast with what might be called an efficiency theory, which holds that concentration arises out of a competitive process in which more-efficient firms grow large and less-efficient firms withdraw or fail. Lack of entry into a concentrated industry, according to this theory, is due to the superior efficiency of large firms, which allows them to sell at prices unattractive to potential entrants. If this is correct, then government policies designed to restructure concentrated industries would lead to less-efficient production and higher prices for consumers.[9]

Concentration and Efficiency

Although much attention has been focused on the profitability of industries at different levels of concentration in order to confirm or refute the shared monopoly theory, little work has been done to measure relative efficiency at different levels of concentration. One exception is a study by Sam Peltzman, in which both the cost-reducing and the profit-raising potentials of industry concentration are considered.[10] He found that the cost-reducing effect of concentration more than offset any profit-raising effect, so the net result of high concentration was lower prices. He concluded that a policy of forced divestiture which reduced the share of the four leading firms in concentrated industries to 50 percent would increase industry costs by about 20 percent and prices by about 10 to 15 percent.[11]

A study by Betty Bock and Jack Farkas of the National Conference Board, which was also focused on the efficiency aspects of concentration, revealed that in most industries output per unit of labor input is higher for the biggest firms than for the rest of the firms in that industry. Their conclusion suggests that leading firms obtain and maintain their large market shares because they use labor resources efficiently. Thus, concentration is a byproduct of efficiency.

Some have argued that the measures used by Bock and Farkas—value added and value of shipments per employee and per production worker–hour—reflect monopoly power to set higher prices as well as efficiency and are, therefore, inappropriate. Bock and Farkas, however, found larger shipments and value added per employee and per production worker–hour in the largest firms in almost *all* industries, not just those industries in which large firms might have market power. Using data from the 1963 Census of Manufactures, they found that in 81 percent of the 345 industries they examined

> the *top-four* companies were at least 5 percent more productive than other companies in the same industry, while in only 5 percent of the industries were the top-four companies definitely less productive than others in the same industry. And again in approximately one-fourth of the industries, the top-four companies accounted for at least 55 percent more value added per production worker man–hour than the remaining companies in the same industry.[12]

The authors reached similar conclusions using value of shipments per employee and value added per production worker–hour. They were not able, however, to examine output per unit of capital, which may be higher for the smallest firms. If so, the findings of Bock and Farkas may reflect a difference in factor proportions between large and small firms that is due to differences in factor costs. Large firms may be more capital-intensive because their cost of capital, compared to that of labor, is lower. Lower risks incurred by investors in large firms and economies of scale in raising capital are likely explanations of a lower relative cost of capital.

Leonard Weiss's study of suboptimal plant capacity adds evidence of greater production efficiency among concentrated industries.[13] He examined the extent to which the capacity of production facilities in various industries was smaller than that necessary to attain the lowest average production cost. He found that suboptimal or high-cost plant capacity was more frequent in unconcentrated than in concentrated industries. In fact, his computations indicate that for every increase of one percentage point in the concentration ratio, the percentage of industry shipments from suboptimal plants declines by 0.86 percent.

Summary of Findings

The study reported in the following pages analyzes *changes* in productivity and price levels in U.S. manufacturing industries that have accompanied *changes* in seller concentration during the last quarter century. Thus, the analysis presented here adds another dimension— that of time—to the work done by Bock and Farkas. In addition, it addresses the issue of the way changes in price are related to changes in concentration.

The evidence presented below refutes the monopoly theory and supports the efficiency theory. If the monopoly theory were correct, when seller concentration increased, productivity would not increase but prices would; but this study demonstrates that industries with rising concentration are marked by greater productivity and lower prices. It suggests that enactment of legislation whose aim is the deconcentration of major manufacturing industries will have harmful effects on both national output and consumer prices.

The first section of this study examines the arguments that concentration is harmful. The second discusses the way in which productivity and price changes were measured. The third reports how price and productivity behaved for different changes in concentration.

Notes

1. Concentration ratios vary among industries in different countries. The reasons include size of market, age of major firms, the technology that they use, and government antitrust policy. The basic patterns of concentration, however, are remarkably similar. For comparisons of concentration ratios among countries, see Joe S. Bain, *International Differences in Industrial Structure* (New Haven, Conn.: Yale University Press, 1966); and F. L. Pryor, "An International Comparison of Concentration Ratios," *Review of Economics and Statistics*, vol. 54 (May 1972), pp. 130–40.

2. F. Bateman and L. Weiss, "Market Structure before the Age of Big Business: Concentration and Profit in Early Southern Manufacturing," *Business History Review*, vol. 49 (Autumn 1975), pp. 312–36.

3. U.S. Congress, House, Committee on Banking and Currency, *Investigation of Financial and Monetary Conditions in the United States*, 62d Cong., 3d sess., 1913.

4. U.S. Congress, Senate, Temporary National Economic Committee, *Final Report and Recommendations*, 77th Cong., 1st sess., 1941, S. Doc. 35.

5. P. C. Neal et al., "Report of the White House Task Force on Antitrust Policy," *Antitrust Law and Economics Review*, vol. 2 (Winter 1968–69), pp. 1–64.

6. U.S. Congress, Senate, *Congressional Record*, 92d Cong., 2d sess., 1972, pp. S11494–99.

7. "Although there are many oligopoly theories, virtually all of them predict an increase in the effectiveness of collusion (a decrease in the cost of collusion) as concentration rises." A. D. Strickland and L. W. Weiss, "Advertising, Concentration and Price-Cost Margins," *Journal of Political Economy*, vol. 84 (October 1976), p. 1113. See also E. H. Chamberlin, *The Theory of Monopolistic Competition* (Cambridge: Harvard University Press, 1933), p. 48, and William Fellner, *Competition among the Few* (New York: Alfred A. Knopf, 1949).

8. For one view of the importance of mergers in attaining monopoly, see George Stigler, "The Statistics of Monopoly and Merger," *Journal of Political Economy*, vol. 64 (February 1956), pp. 33–40, and his "Mergers and Preventive Antitrust Policy," *University of Pennsylvania Law Review*, vol. 104, no. 2 (November 1955), pp. 176–84. In the latter, Stigler states, "A preventive antitrust policy . . . should be directed at activities which on their face have a general and important tendency to reduce competition and only at such activities. Mergers of business rivals are unique in the degree to which they meet this requirement . . . . This is, indeed, their chief purpose: historically the other purposes of mergers (of large firms) have been incidental and unimportant" (p. 177).

9. John McGee, *In Defense of Industrial Concentration* (New York: Praeger Publishers, 1971).

10. Sam Peltzman, "The Gains and Losses from Industrial Concentration," *Journal of Law and Economics*, vol. 20 (October 1977), pp. 53–100. See also J.H. Landon, "The Relation of Market Concentration to Advertising Rate: The Newspaper Industry," *The Antitrust Bulletin*, vol. 16 (1971), pp. 53–100.

11. Peltzman, "Gains and Losses," p. 263.

12. Betty Bock and Jack Farkas, *Concentration and Productivity: Some Preliminary Problems and Findings* (New York: The Conference Board, 1969), p. 23. Emphasis in original. Similar findings, based on data for 1972, were reported by Edward Miller, "The Extent of Economies of Scale: The Effects of Firm Size on Labor Productivity and Wage Rates," *Southern Economic Journal*, vol. 44 (January 1978), pp. 470–87.

13. Leonard Weiss, "Optimal Plant Size and the Extent of Suboptimal Capacity," in *Essays on Industrial Organization in Honor of Joe S. Bain*, ed. Robert Masson and David Qualls (Cambridge, Mass.: Ballinger, 1976), pp. 123–41.

6

2
Arguments That Concentration Is Harmful

The postulated harm to consumers from high concentration supposedly stems from the possibility that competition among a small number of sellers will not force prices down to their resource cost. Where a few firms account for the bulk of industry output, collusion (tacit or overt) among them to raise prices becomes easier. Even in the absence of economies of scale, therefore, firms may grow large through mergers or internal expansion in order to facilitate collusion. Some even argue that mergers have been the main road to large firm size (relative to the size of the industry) and that the main purpose of becoming large through mergers has been to attain monopoly or shared monopoly.[1]

This argument ignores the fact that when collusion succeeds in raising industry profits to levels in excess of the cost of capital, new entrants are attracted.[2] As entries occur and output expands, prices decline. Alternatively, to maintain price levels, firms already in an industry must restrict their output as new firms enter, thus earning lower profits because of the costs of carrying excess capacity. Even if the existing firms ultimately acquire the new entrants, other companies will continue to be attracted as long as industry profits are above normal or prices are above the minimum average cost in efficiently scaled and operated businesses. Therefore, in the absence of economies of scale, any increase in profits from mergers resulting in industry concentration is likely to be short-lived.

In 1921 Arthur Dewing studied the profit performance of thirty-five consolidations that had taken place around 1900. Each had united five or more firms that had been competitors. He found that earnings in the ten years following each merger averaged 18 percent less than the total earnings of the constituent firms before the merger.[3] Evidently, entry and expansion by existing firms—including those that had been consolidated—were adequate to keep prices at competitive levels despite the high degree of concentration brought about by the consolidations. The National Industrial Conference Board, in its 1929 study of mergers, found that from 1900 to 1913 prices dropped 13 percent in twenty-six industries in which there were major consolidations, while prices rose 10 percent in thirty-three industries in which only minor consolidations or none occurred.[4]

In response to the argument that new entries ultimately eliminate any profit from collusive agreements, advocates of the monopoly theory assert that barriers to entry allow colluding firms in concentrated industries to maintain high profits. The barriers most often cited are the large capital expenditures required to build plants or to carry out intensive advertising campaigns. Entry on a small scale would presumably be unsuccessful because, in concentrated industries, small firms are less efficient than large firms.[5] Thus, even the advocates of the monopoly theory implicitly concede that economies of scale are a factor underlying concentration. They maintain, however, that while economies of scale are partially responsible for high concentration, existing market shares of large firms are far in excess of what is necessary to realize all these cost savings.[6] Thus, industries could be less concentrated than they now are with no loss of efficiency.

The argument that concentrated industries, such as those producing primary aluminum and automobiles, are protected by capital barriers has intuitive appeal—especially when that situation is contrasted with the situation in industries in which firms are small, such as services or retail trade. After all, almost anyone can buy a restaurant, but only the extremely wealthy can buy steel mills. What this view fails to consider is that the corporate form, by pooling the investments of many people, allows the less wealthy to buy a share of a business they could not enter individually and thereby enables the corporation to assemble the capital required to enter a concentrated industry.

Also, if it is true that firms in concentrated industries generally set prices in a monopolistic fashion, then profits to sellers in most of these industries are higher than those available elsewhere (for the same risk) and are therefore higher than the cost of capital.[7] For that reason, firms in other industries that are large enough to raise capital economically have a great incentive to enter concentrated industries. Chemical companies, for example, could earn higher profits by entering the aluminum industry if it were profitable enough to provide earnings in excess of the cost of capital. Even if chemical companies were already earning excess profits on their investments, existing or potential stockholders would be willing to provide additional funds for their companies to manufacture aluminum if monopoly profits were to be had. The additional returns would provide even higher dividends and capital gains to the stockholders. Alternatively, or as part of their strategy, the chemical companies could borrow at the competitive market rate in the bond market and make profits at a higher rate in the aluminum industry.

A company's incentive to enter an industry that prices its product above competitive levels is much greater when the company uses that industry's product in its production process or when that industry's product complements its own product. Thus, if aluminum companies were obtaining monopoly profits, it would pay automobile companies to enter the aluminum industry, since they could lower their own costs of production. Or, if the major oil companies were monopolistic, it would pay automobile companies to enter the oil industry, since the lower gasoline prices that competition would bring would increase the demand for automobiles. All of this follows if the major barrier to entry into concentrated industries is the inability of new firms to raise capital. And it highlights the weakness of the capital-barriers argument—that potential entrants are unable to raise capital even though investors know they could obtain profits by providing it.

It may be that capital is more difficult to raise in concentrated industries because the risks there are greater. Greater risk in a concentrated industry may be attributable to the fact that its assets are more specialized and more durable than those of other industries. Examples of specialized and durable resources used in concentrated industries are those secured through large expenditures for plant and equipment, advertising campaigns, or research and development (R&D) programs. The use of such resources creates barriers to exit as well as to entry, because specialization limits alternative uses and durability creates sunk costs that restrain exit when the rate of profit falls below expectations. For example, a highly trained and specialized labor force represents human capital; investments in advertising create brand identification, and investments in R&D create new products and technology. Each of these resources is difficult to transfer from one area of economic activity to another. Outlays in these areas become fixed costs, and when these constitute a large portion of total costs, operations often continue despite deficient profits or losses. Thus, resource specialization and durability, which keep potential entrants out of an industry when its profits are abnormally high because of the time it takes to build specialized plants and equipment, also keep existing firms from leaving an industry when its profits are abnormally low.

The inability of some concentrated industries to transfer assets out of particular activities means that investment in these industries is very risky. Investment in specialized plant and equipment or in training workers also has very small liquidation value if the intended use turns out to be unprofitable. Likewise, advertising expenditures rarely have

9

any liquidation value. And investment in R&D to develop a new product that ultimately fails often has no liquidation value. The greater risk involved in using specialized and durable assets means that higher rates of return are necessary to attract capital—that is, the cost of capital is higher in a risky industry. For that reason, the higher rate of profitability sometimes observed in concentrated industries may be a consequence of the greater risk inherent in the types of assets they must use. Entry will not, and should not, occur unless the expected return equals or exceeds the risk-adjusted (higher) cost of capital invested in risky assets.

If it is difficult to transfer resources out of concentrated industries, then firms are deterred from entering if the expected returns do not justify the costs—including the risk of failure—of acquiring and implementing complex technologies. There is no misallocation of resources in this case since, taking the cost of the risk into account, the potential entrants' resources are better used elsewhere.

The differences that exist in the average rate of profitability between concentrated and unconcentrated industries are perhaps explained by differences in risk.[8] But the more important question to be answered is whether concentration is related to the efficiency of an industry. Profits may be higher either because costs are lower or because prices are higher. When concentration increases, consumers can be better off even if profits are higher, if the greater profits are realized from reductions in cost that lead to reductions in selling prices.

In the balance of this study two questions are examined. First, are the prevailing levels of industry concentration explained by efficiency factors or could firms be smaller than they are now with no loss in efficiency? Second, are any of the gains from growth in productivity that are attributable to high concentration passed on to consumers through reduced selling prices? The first question will be addressed by tracing changes in productivity as industries moved to their current level of concentration. The second will be addressed by determining the extent to which prices fell as concentration changed.

Notes

1. George Stigler, "Mergers and Preventive Antitrust Policy," *University of Pennsylvania Law Review*, vol. 104, no. 2 (November 1955), p. 177.

2. For examples of industries in which this has been the case, see Fritz Voight, "German Experience with Cartels and Their Control during Pre-war and Post-war Periods," in *Competition, Cartels and Their Regulation*, ed. J. Miller (Amsterdam: North-Holland, 1962), pp. 169–213.

3. A. S. Dewing, "A Statistical Test of the Success of Consolidations," *Quarterly Journal of Economics*, vol. 36 (November 1921), pp. 81–101.

4. National Industrial Conference Board, *Mergers in Industry* (New York, 1929), pp. 143–46.

5. See Harold Demsetz, "Industry Structure, Market Rivalry, and Public Policy," *Journal of Law and Economics*, vol. 16 (1973), pp. 1–10, and John R. Carter, "Collusion, Efficiency, and Antitrust," *Journal of Law and Economics*, vol. 21 (1978), pp. 435–44.

6. Joe S. Bain, "Economies of Scale, Concentration and the Condition of Entry in Twenty Manufacturing Industries," *American Economic Review*, vol. 44 (March 1954), pp. 15–39.

7. Of course, monopoly power does not guarantee higher-than-normal returns on invested capital. Some monopolists earn less than their cost of capital and eventually leave their industries. Subnormal returns could persist for some time when company assets are durable and specialized, with the consequence that they have few alternative uses outside their current employment.

8. David Qualls has found evidence that price-cost margins are more variable in concentrated industries, implying higher firm-specific risk. David Qualls, "Market Structure and the Cyclical Flexibility of Price-Cost Margins," *Journal of Business*, vol. 52 (April 1979), pp. 305–25.

3
Measuring Growth in Productivity

Productivity may be defined as the ratio of output to input. Growth in productivity is therefore the change in this ratio in time. The greater the growth in output in relation to the growth in input, the greater the growth in productivity. Measurement of productivity, however, is complicated by the fact that usually several types of inputs—labor and capital, for example—are used to produce one output. In order to compute growth in productivity, therefore, one must measure the growth of each of the inputs—unless it is known that all inputs grow at the same rate. When they grow at different rates, an average of all the input growth rates must be computed and compared to the growth rate of output. In the tables that follow, growth in productivity is computed as the ratio of the growth of output to a geometrically weighted average growth of inputs, where the weights are the average shares of each factor in the industry's value added.

For this study, two measures of productivity were computed for each industry. The first, designated total factor productivity, takes account of both capital and labor factors of production. The second, designated labor productivity, includes only the labor inputs for production and nonproduction workers. The latter implicitly assumes that the growth of the excluded factors is the same as that of the included factors. The labor productivity measure was used because labor inputs are more easily and accurately measured than capital inputs. To the extent that capital inputs grow faster or slower than labor inputs, the labor productivity measure overstates or understates the true gains in efficiency. Despite the potential differences, the two measures of productivity were in fact highly correlated ($r = 0.78$).

The measurement of the output of an industry is based on indexes of production compiled for Standard Industrial Classification (SIC) four-digit industries by the Federal Reserve Board of Governors and the U.S. Bureau of the Census for those years in which a census of manufactures was conducted.[1] These are the bench-mark indexes used by the Federal Reserve Board and the U.S. Bureau of Labor Statistics to adjust their monthly indexes of industrial output. The bench-marks are constructed by using a price index to deflate the value of shipments for each five-digit class of products within a four-digit industry and then aggregating across product classes using product value-added weights. The result is an index that represents annual real value added in each industry during the census years.

The data on labor inputs, factor shares, and market structure are derived from the industry statistics published in the Census of Manufactures for various years between 1947 and 1972 and from tables of concentration ratios that were published as part of the census or as separate reports. The data on capital inputs were taken from J. W. Kendrick's compilation for two-digit manufacturing industries.[2] Appendix A contains a detailed description of the computation of total factor and labor productivity measures and the method used here for computing price changes.

Two measures of change in industry structure were also computed. The first, the absolute change in the four-firm concentration ratio, is the increase or decrease for the period in the share of domestic output accounted for by the four largest firms in the industry. The second, the ratio of the number of firms in the industry at the end of the period to the number of firms at the beginning of the period, is a measure of net entry (when the ratio is greater than one) or net exit (when the ratio is less than one).

The Significance of Relative Growth in Productivity and Changes in Price

The purpose of examining the behavior of productivity growth and price change for industries with different changes in concentration or different rates of net entry or exit is to test the efficiency and monopoly theories of concentration. If concentration increased in an industry because the most efficient firms grew faster than the others in the industry or because inefficient smaller companies left the industry, then growth in productivity should be highest in industries where concentration increased most or the decrease in the number of firms was greatest. If the gains in productivity were passed on to consumers through lower prices, then price increases should be smallest in industries where concentration increased most or the number of firms decreased most. If, however, increasing concentration is primarily the result of efforts to attain monopoly power, then productivity growth should be unrelated to changes in concentration or number of firms, and price increases should be greatest where industry concentration increased most or the number of firms decreased most. A price increase would result if increased concentration did not lead to greater efficiency but made it easier for the firms to collude, and the firms in

13

fact did collude. This would be the case if small firms left the industry because of predatory pricing or other "monopolizing" business practices rather than because they were less efficient than the larger firms.

It should be kept in mind that many proponents of the monopoly theory argue that economies of scale are part of the reason for concentration. They contend that economies of scale may require some firms to be large, but not as large as they are now. Thus, most highly concentrated industries could be less concentrated than they are without sacrificing economies of scale. The monopoly theorists imply that moderate decreases in concentration from a high level would have no effect on productivity.

Since most of the major changes in market structure took place well before World War II, the changes in concentration measured in this study, which covers the period 1947–1972, can be considered marginal changes. The following analysis of changes in productivity and prices with respect to changes in concentration, therefore, provides an appropriate test of the monopoly theory, even in its more moderate form.

Notes

1. U.S. Bureau of the Census and Board of Governors of the Federal Reserve System, *Census of Manufactures, 1963*, vol. 4 (1968); U.S. Bureau of the Census, *Census of Manufactures and Mineral Industries, 1967*, Special Report Series: Indexes of Production (MC67 (s)) - 6 (1975); and U.S. Bureau of the Census, *Census of Manufactures, 1972*, vol. 4 (1977).

2. J. W. Kendrick, *Post War Productivity Trends in the United States 1948–69* (New York: National Bureau of Economic Research, 1973), and Conference Board, *The National Wealth of the United States by Major Sectors and Industry* (New York, 1976).

4
Growth in Productivity and Changes in Price, 1947–1972

In table 2 growth in productivity and changes in price that accompanied different changes in concentration are compared for the periods 1947–1972 and 1954–1972. Changes in industrial structure generally occur slowly, particularly in industries with long-lived assets, so a substantial period is required to measure their effects accurately. Since the period 1947–1972 is longer, it is more appropriate for determining the ultimate effect of changes in concentration on productivity growth. The data for that period, however, suffer from two faults: First, the number of industries for which both 1947 and 1972 data are available is small; and, second, the data on the growth of capital inputs used in measuring productivity are less reliable for 1947–1972 than for 1954–1972 (see appendix A). For these reasons the analysis below covers both periods.

The Effects of Changes in Concentration

The entries in table 2 are unweighted average annual rates of total factor productivity growth, labor productivity growth, and price changes for four classes of industries. The Census Bureau collects data on more than four hundred manufacturing industries defined at the four-digit level of aggregation—the most disaggregated level at which productivity can be measured. In assembling the data for this study, however, many industries were excluded for one or more of the following reasons: The industry definition changed between census years; the concentration ratio was not published, generally because of disclosure restrictions; and data on one or more inputs or outputs were not available for either the beginning or the ending census years. (For a more detailed description of the computation of the variables in table 2 and for some of the limitations of the underlying data, see appendixes A and B.)

The classes in table 2 were determined on the basis of the change in the four-firm industry concentration ratio—that is, the change in the

TABLE 2

AVERAGE ANNUAL GROWTH IN PRODUCTIVITY AND CHANGES IN PRICE,
ACCORDING TO INCREASING OR DECREASING INDUSTRY CONCENTRATION, 1947–1972 AND 1954–1972

Variable	Decreases in Concentration			Increases in Concentration			All Industries
	12 percent or more (Class I)	Less than 12 percent or no change (Class II)	All decreases (Classes I and II)	12 percent or less (Class III)	More than 12 percent (Class IV)	All increases (Classes III and IV)	
				1947–1972			
Percent annual growth in total productivity	1.93	1.80	1.84	1.86	2.30	2.03	1.95
Number of industries	20	41	61	47	29	76	137
				1954–1972			
Percent annual growth in total productivity	2.57	1.84	2.01	1.96	2.71	2.12	2.08
Number of industries	15	48	63	77	22	99	162
				1947–1972			
Percent annual growth in labor productivity	2.79	2.82	2.81	2.65	3.23	2.87	2.84
Number of industries	20	41	61	47	29	76	137

Percent annual growth in labor productivity	3.64	2.69	2.92	3.01	3.81	3.19	3.08
Number of industries	15	48	63	77	22	99	162
				1954–1972			
Percent change in price[a]	2.10	2.19	2.16	2.16	1.98	2.09	2.12
Number of industries	20	41	61	47	29	76	137
				1947–1972			
Percent change in price[a]	1.47	2.16	2.00	2.10	1.84	2.04	2.02
Number of industries	15	48	63	77	22	99	162
				1954–1972			

NOTE: For all classes, mean change in concentration for 1947–1972 = 2.2, s.d. = 12.8; for all classes mean change in concentration for 1954–1972 = 2.3, s.d. = 10.3.
a. Nominal changes in price are used.
SOURCE: Appendix B.

percentage market share of the four largest sellers. Classes I and II contain industries in which concentration decreased, while Classes III and IV contain industries in which concentration increased. Class I includes only the industries with decreases of twelve percentage points or more; Class II, those with declines of less than twelve points or none at all; Class III, those with increases of twelve points or less; and Class IV, those with increases of more than twelve points.

Table 2 reveals several important patterns. First, industries with rising concentration ratios generally showed greater increases in productivity than those with declining ratios. Also, their price increases were roughly equal to or smaller than those in industries with declining concentration ratios. In the period 1947–1972, the average annual rate of increase in total productivity was 1.84 percent for those industries in which concentration declined and 2.03 percent for those in which concentration increased. This represents a cumulative difference for the twenty-five year period of 7.5 percent. In the same period, price level changes for industries with rising concentration were 0.07 percent a year lower or 2.9 percent cumulatively.

The second important pattern is that the highest rate of growth in productivity occurred in those industries in which the increase in concentration was greatest. For 1947–1972, the rate of total factor growth in productivity for Class IV was 2.30 percent a year, while the average for all other industries was 1.85 percent a year. This amounts to a cumulative difference of 18.8 percent for the period. Class IV also had the lowest rate of increase in prices for this period. The differences between the rate of price increases for Class IV and the average for all other classes was 0.18 percent a year or 7.4 percent cumulatively. The data for 1954–1972, which are based on a larger sample of industries, show the same pattern of superior performance for those industries with the largest increases in concentration.

The third important pattern in table 2 is the evidence of superior productivity and price performance for industries with large decreases in concentration compared with industries with moderate increases or moderate decreases. In both periods the rate of growth in productivity of Class I was higher than that of either Class II or Class III. This pattern suggests that large decreases, as well as increases, in concentration are associated with efficiency. This trend is consistent with a theory that changes in concentration are related to changes in efficiency and in this context implies that technological innovations can be scale reducing as well as scale increasing. That is, cost-saving innovations at times can be better suited to smaller firms and could reduce or even eliminate the cost advantage of the largest firms, thus leading to both reduced concentration and greater efficiency of the industry. In some instances

18

it may be small or medium-sized firms that benefit most from innovation. If small or medium-sized firms expanded their share of the market but did not overtake the leading firms or if they displaced leading firms without growing as large relative to the industry as the former leading firms, decreases in concentration and increases in productivity would occur at the same time.

The higher rate of growth in productivity among the industries with the largest decreases in concentration could also be the result of industry growth that allows the smaller firms to attain the minimum efficient scale. If further expansion of the largest firms leads to higher production costs—that is, if the long-run average-cost curve is U shaped—then industry growth should allow the smallest firms to increase their share of industry output, which would in turn lead to high growth in productivity and decreases in concentration.

The pattern of higher productivity growth for large increases and large decreases in concentration may seem somewhat contradictory. It merely suggests, however, that long-term changes in the structure of an industry in either direction are the result of market forces that lead to greater efficiency. This pattern indicates that some industries are most efficient with an atomistic structure while others are most efficient with an oligopolistic structure.

In addition, table 2 reveals that the differences in growth of productivity between classes are larger than the differences in price changes, which implies that increases in concentration led to higher wages for labor or to higher profits for owners of firms or both.[1] Thus, there seems to be some support for the contention that concentration allows firms to increase their profits by colluding.[2] The data reveal, however, that the source of what may be higher profits was lower costs through greater productivity rather than collusion to raise prices. Prices were substantially lower to consumers because of the superior productivity that accompanied increasing concentration. Consumers benefited when concentration rose and the rise was accompanied by greater-than-average increases in productivity.

Unfortunately, the data in table 2 do not allow the determination of the exact source of the growth in productivity that accompanied increased concentration. There are several possibilities. One is that greater concentration resulted from horizontal mergers that allowed firms to benefit from economies of scale. Throughout most of the period covered by this study, however, horizontal mergers were severely restricted by the antitrust laws. Thus, increased concentration outside atomistic industries probably came about through internal expansion of some firms and contraction or exit of others.

Although this study stresses the presence of economies of scale as

19

a reason for concentration, the relationship observed between concentration and productivity could come about even in their absence.[3] One possible way this could happen, Peltzman proposed, is through the expansion of more efficient firms.[4] Peltzman suggested that, with the passage of time, some firms discover productive techniques which are not easily imitated by rivals, while others are slow to introduce techniques already widely adopted in their industry. Thus, the most progressive firms expand their share of the market while the least progressive lose theirs. If the former are already among the four largest in the industry, the industry four-firm concentration ratio will increase as the productivity of the industry increases. Concentration changes will then correlate positively with changes in productivity. If the most progressive firms are not among the four largest, however, and do not expand enough to enter that group, the concentration ratio will decrease as the productivity of the industry increases. Concentration and change in productivity will, then, correlate negatively. But if across industries progressiveness is random—that is, if in some industries small firms tend to be more progressive while in others large firms are more progressive—then growth in productivity will be related to the absolute magnitude of concentration change. In that case, the largest changes in concentration would accompany the greatest growth in productivity, and these would be increases as often as decreases.

Peltzman found that while growth in productivity was related to the absolute magnitude of the change in concentration, the relation was much stronger in the case of increasing concentration. The data in table 2 also show that the dominant relation is between increases in concentration and increases in productivity. But there is also evidence to support Peltzman's hypothesis that large decreases in concentration are also associated with large increases in productivity.

Entry and Exit Rates

Entry into or exit from an industry can affect the productivity of the industry if the entering or exiting firms are more (or less) efficient than the rest of the industry. In table 3, average annual rates of productivity growth and changes in price levels are compared for industries with different rates of change in the number of sellers and of industry growth. An increase in the number of sellers is labeled "net entry" (Classes I and II) and a decrease is labeled "net exit" (Classes III and IV).

All Industries. When the behavior of all industries regardless of industry growth is examined, the patterns in table 3 appear to be

TABLE 3

AVERAGE ANNUAL GROWTH IN PRODUCTIVITY AND CHANGES IN PRICE IN INDUSTRIES CLASSIFIED BY RATE OF NET ENTRY OR EXIT AND BY REAL GROWTH RATE, 1947–1972 AND 1954–1972

| | Net Entry | | | Net Exit | | |
Variable and Growth Rate[a]	Increase of more than 60 percent (Class I)	Increase of 60 percent or less (Class II)	All increases (Classes I and II)	Decrease of less than 30 percent (Class III)	Decrease of 30 percent or more (Class IV)	All decreases (Classes III and IV)
			1947–1972			
All industries						
Percent annual growth in productivity[b]	2.18	1.68	1.90	1.95	2.01	1.99
Percent change in price	2.36	2.29	2.32	1.99	1.90	1.93
Number of industries	30	37	77	26	44	70
High-growth industries						
Percent annual growth in productivity	2.35	2.56	2.42	2.55	3.56	3.07
Percent change in price	2.28	1.87	2.12	1.80	0.81	1.28
Number of industries	27	17	44	12	13	25
Low-growth industries						
Percent annual growth in productivity	0.64	0.93	0.89	1.43	1.36	1.38
Percent change in price	3.16	2.64	2.71	2.15	2.35	2.29
Number of industries	3	20	23	14	31	45

(Table continues)

TABLE 3 (continued)

Variable and Growth Rate[a]	Net Entry			Net Exit		
	Increase of more than 60 percent (Class I)	Increase of 60 percent or less (Class II)	All increases (Classes I and II)	Decrease of less than 30 percent (Class III)	Decrease of 30 percent or more (Class IV)	All decreases (Classes III and IV)
			1954–1972			
All industries						
Percent annual growth in productivity	2.70	1.89	2.15	2.16	1.93	2.02
Percent change in price	1.59	2.19	1.99	2.07	2.04	1.47
Number of industries	22	45	67	40	54	94
High-growth industries						
Percent annual growth in productivity	2.89	2.35	2.57	2.65	3.58	2.99
Percent change in price	1.42	1.98	2.57	1.76	1.20	1.28
Number of industries	19	26	45	23	13	25
Low-growth industries						
Percent annual growth in productivity	1.51	1.26	1.30	1.51	1.41	1.43
Percent change in price	2.65	2.47	2.49	2.49	2.30	2.35
Number of industries	3	19	22	17	41	58

a. Growth is classified as high if it is higher than the median industry growth rate and low if it is lower than the median industry growth rate. The median for 1947–1972 was 3.0 percent a year; the median for 1954–1972 was 3.2 percent a year.
b. Growth in productivity refers to growth in total factor productivity.
SOURCE: Appendix B.

mixed. The highest growth in productivity was among industries with the greatest increases in their number of constituent firms (Class I). Those industries with the greatest decreases in number of firms (Class IV) had the second highest productivity growth for 1947–1972 and the third highest for 1954–1972.

According to the efficiency theory, exiting firms ought to be the least efficient and growth in productivity ought to be greatest where exits are most numerous. The highest growth in productivity, however, was among industries in which *entries* were greatest. Industries with the greatest decrease in number of firms had only the second greatest growth in productivity for 1947–1972 and the third highest growth in productivity for 1954–1972. Thus there seems to be little support here for the efficiency theory. The monopoly theory predicts the greatest price increase where the decline in the number of firms is greatest, because the ability to collude is enhanced. But the lowest rate of price increase for 1947–1972 and second lowest for 1954–1972 was in this group of industries (Class IV). Thus, table 3 provides little support for the monopoly theory.

Industries Classified According to Growth in Output. Industry growth, which is generally associated with increases in productivity,[5] is also associated with increases in the number of firms. Part of the higher productivity associated with net entry, therefore, could be the result of industry growth. Both industry growth and changes in the number of sellers affect increases in the size of firms, which may influence productivity because of economies of scale. If industry growth is high, average firm size may increase despite an increase in the number of sellers. In analyzing the effect of entry on productivity, therefore, the simultaneous effects of industry growth had to be taken into account. To do this, industries were classified as high-growth industries when their growth rates were above the median for all industries and as low-growth industries otherwise. The results are also in table 3.

Evaluating the effects of entry by separating high-growth and low-growth industries yields results that are consistent with those of table 2 and are even more striking. Table 3 reveals that for both the high-growth and the low-growth groups increases in productivity were greater and price increases smaller in industries with net exit than for those with net entry. The differences were greatest in high-growth industries. In the period 1947–1972, for high-growth industries, the rate of growth in productivity for Classes III and IV (net exit) combined was 3.07 percent a year, while it was only 2.42 percent for Classes I and II (net entry) combined. This amounts to a cumulative difference of

31.2 percent. At the same time, the rate of price increase was 1.28 percent a year for Classes III and IV and 2.12 percent for Classes I and II. The cumulative difference amounts to price increases 31.5 percent lower in industries with net exit.[6]

Table 3 also shows that those industries in which the decline in the number of firms was greatest (Class IV), the rate of growth in productivity was highest and the rate of price increase was smallest. This was true of high-growth industries in both periods and of low-growth industries in one period. For 1947–1972, among high-growth industries, the differences in growth in productivity between Class IV and the average of Classes I and II combined was 1.14 percent a year. This amounts to a cumulative difference of 58 percent. At the same time the cumulative price increase was 47 percent lower for Class IV than the average of Classes I and II combined.[7]

There is also some indication that for the period 1954–1972, in industries in which increases in the number of firms were large, increases in productivity were higher than in industries in which increases in the number of firms were moderate. This is consistent with the evidence in table 2 and suggests that cost-saving innovations which give an advantage to smaller firms generally lead to their entry.

In sum, an analysis of the data on changes in the number of sellers presented in table 3 provides results consistent with the analysis of changes in concentration presented in table 2. It suggests that greater growth in productivity and smaller increases in prices, particularly in industries with high rates of growth, have accompanied reductions in the number of sellers as a result of mergers or exits of less efficient firms.

The Role of Industry Growth

Because the analysis presented in table 2 does not explicitly consider growth, the differences in increases in productivity and changes in price between the classes are rather moderate. Growth is related to productivity in two important ways. First, high growth speeds the introduction of cost-saving technology whenever it is embodied in new plant and equipment. Without growth, new techniques may be introduced only as old plant and equipment deteriorate and are replaced. The rate of growth in productivity in response to innovation is therefore likely to be slower in the absence of growth in the industry. The second reason that industry growth is important is that it may itself be a result of a cost-saving innovation which allows firms to reduce prices and which increases the quantity of output that consumers wish to purchase. Industry growth is thus a determinant of productivity as well as an indication that productivity has increased.

Concentration is also influenced by industry growth. A high rate of growth facilitates new entry by reducing the share of the market needed to attain the most efficient scale of production. As is apparent from table 3, a high rate of growth is more often associated with increases than with decreases in the number of firms. Therefore growth is generally associated with decreasing concentration. Since growth increases productivity but also reduces concentration, failure to control for industry growth when studying the relation between concentration and productivity will lead to biased results. Any positive correlation between concentration and productivity can be attenuated by the influence of growth.

In table 4 the rate of growth in productivity and changes in price are shown for industries grouped into the same four classes of concentration change used in table 2 and also into two growth classes divided at the median real growth rate of all industries. The table shows that industries with the higher growth rates for output did show a higher rate of growth in productivity. For 1947–1972, the average rate of increase in productivity in the high-growth industries was more than twice that in the low-growth industries.

Table 4 also shows that the relations between growth in productivity, changes in prices, and changes in concentration shown in table 2 are much stronger in high-growth industries. During the period 1947–1972, productivity in this group grew 2.26 percent a year in industries in which concentration was decreasing and 3.22 percent in those in which concentration was increasing. Prices increased 2.05 percent a year among the former and 1.55 percent among the latter.[8] Cumulatively, growth in productivity for the period was 46 percent higher and price increases 19 percent lower in industries in which concentration was increasing.

With high growth, industries with the largest decreases in concentration (Class I) showed higher growth in productivity than those in which decreases in concentration were moderate (Class II). A better estimate of the effect of rising concentration can therefore be obtained by comparing Classes II and IV. Here the difference in the annual rate of growth in productivity for 1947–1972 was 1.33 percent and the difference in the rate of price change was 0.68 percent. Cumulatively, productivity grew 64 percent more and prices rose 26 percent less among industries in which increases in concentration were largest. For the period 1954–1972, the difference was 1.69 percent a year in productivity and 0.92 percent in prices.[9] A more sophisticated estimate of the behavior of productivity over the range of concentration changes

TABLE 4

AVERAGE ANNUAL RATES OF GROWTH IN PRODUCTIVITY AND CHANGES IN PRICE IN HIGH- AND LOW-GROWTH INDUSTRIES

Variable and Growth Rate[a]	Concentration Decreases			Concentration Increases			All Industries
	12 percent or more (Class I)	Less than 12 percent or no change (Class II)	All decreases (Classes I and II)	12 percent or less (Class III)	More than 12 percent (Class IV)	All increases (Classes III and IV)	
				1947–1972			
High-growth industries							
Percent annual growth in productivity[b]	2.66	2.09	2.26	3.10	3.42	3.22	2.70
Percent change in price	1.71	2.19	2.05	1.58	1.51	1.55	1.82
Number of industries	11	26	37	20	11	31	68
Low-growth industries							
Percent annual growth in productivity	1.03	1.30	1.20	0.94	1.61	1.21	1.21
Percent change in price	2.58	2.19	2.34	2.59	2.27	2.46	2.42
Number of industries	9	15	24	27	18	45	69

1954–1972

High-growth industries							
Percent annual growth in productivity	3.10	2.17	2.43	2.78	3.86	3.06	2.76
Percent change in price	0.75	2.19	1.78	1.65	1.27	1.55	1.66
Number of industries	11	28	39	31	11	42	81
Low-growth industries							
Percent annual growth in productivity	1.10	1.37	1.32	1.40	1.56	1.43	1.40
Percent change in price	3.44	2.13	2.35	2.41	2.40	2.41	2.39
Number of industries	4	20	24	46	11	57	81

a. Growth is classified as high if it is higher than the median industry growth rate and low if it is lower than the median industry growth rate. The median for 1947–1972 was 3.0 percent a year; the median for 1954–1972 was 3.2 percent a year.
b. Growth in productivity refers to growth in total factor productivity.
SOURCE: Appendix B.

can be made using least squares regression analysis. This is discussed in appendix A.

Another way of assessing the effect of concentration is to compare industries in which increases were greatest in concentration (Class IV) to all industries in which concentration decreased (the average of Classes I and II combined). Growth in productivity was higher in Class IV by 1.16 and 1.43 percent a year in 1947–1972 and 1954–1972, respectively; at the same time, price changes were lower by 0.54 and 0.51 percent.[10]

Among the low-growth industries, the pattern of productivity and price change was generally the same as that of the high-growth industries, but the differences between the groups were much smaller. An important difference between low-growth and high-growth industries appears in the behavior of Class I. For high-growth industries, Class I outperformed Class II with higher growth in productivity and smaller price increases. Among low-growth industries, however, Class I showed poorer performance in productivity and prices than Class II. For 1947–1972, growth in productivity in Class I was 0.27 percent a year lower and price change was higher by 0.39 percent a year. These results indicate that large decreases in concentration lead to greater growth in productivity *only* in the presence of industry growth, which is consistent with the theory that high growth in an industry allows the small or medium-sized firms to expand and to realize economies of scale otherwise available only to the large firms.

There are several other ways to account for the different effects of concentration change on growth in productivity in high-growth and low-growth industries. The larger effect of concentration on productivity in the case of high growth can be explained in part by noting that, since growth increases productivity in all industries, differences among the concentration classes ought to be proportionately higher. The rate of change in productivity was about twice as large in all high-growth industries as in all low-growth industries, while the magnitude of the differences between the concentration classes was four or five times that in the low-growth industries. It appears, then, that growth in an industry magnifies the effect of a change in concentration on productivity out of proportion to the general influence of growth on productivity.

The explanation for this interaction may be related to a process of self-selection. As stated earlier, growth in an industry is generally associated with declines in concentration, because growth reduces the share of the market that a firm must attain to achieve an efficient scale of production. If concentration in an industry rises despite high growth, it suggests that significant technological changes have taken

28

place which were adopted more quickly by larger firms or which made the larger firms more efficient.[11] Low or negative growth, however, could signify a mature or declining industry which firms are leaving, thereby increasing the concentration of sellers, although no technological change has occurred. The absence of technological change may even be a reason for the industry's decline. Thus, in the case of high growth, *increases* in concentration are more likely to be the result of technological advance that has increased the minimum efficient firm size and that should be accompanied by substantial growth in productivity. But in the case of low or negative growth, changes in concentration in an industry might be associated with only small increases in productivity, since such changes in productivity come about when firms that may be only marginally less efficient than the remaining firms exit.

The results in table 4 give more support to Peltzman's empirical findings than did my earlier analysis of this topic.[12] In that paper I confirmed Peltzman's finding on increasing concentration but disputed his observation that decreasing concentration could increase growth in productivity. It is apparent from table 4 and a plot of concentration and productivity presented in appendix A that while moderate declines in concentration among high-growth industries are associated with lower productivity, large declines are associated with higher productivity. There is also evidence here of the growth interaction observed by Peltzman but disputed in my earlier analysis.

Notes

1. It is possible that the differences between price and productivity reflect inaccuracies in the measurement of productivity that have led to an overstatement of its growth. One source of bias may be the omission of intangible capital which may increase with increases in concentration. Or it may be that the higher profits represent a temporary disequilibrium effect related to whatever factors are responsible for the concentration increase (for example, successful innovation).

2. Increased concentration may make collusion easier.

3. Economies of scale refer to the lower costs attained by larger firms.

4. Sam Peltzman, "The Gains and Losses from Industrial Concentration," *Journal of Law and Economics*, vol. 20 (October 1977), pp. 231–33.

5. George Stigler, in a sample of 29 industries whose growth in productivity was measured for the period 1899–1937, found that in industries in which there was a large decrease in concentration, the growth in output was five times as great and the increase in productivity was twice as great as in industries in which the concentration did not change. George Stigler, "Industrial Organization and Economic Progress," in Leonard White, ed., *The State of the Social Sciences* (Chicago: University of Chicago Press, 1956), p. 278.

6. To verify the statistical significance of these differences, t tests were performed on the average for Classes I and II combined compared with the average of Classes III and IV combined. For growth in productivity the t value was 1.72 and for price change the t

value was 2.46. These values are significant at the 0.04 and 0.01 levels, respectively. The significance levels are one-tailed tests and were computed using a pooled variance estimate, since F tests on the group variances indicated no group differences. The 0.04 significance level means that, were there really no differences between the classes, the probability is only four chances in a hundred that the average rate of growth in productivity of Classes III and IV combined would exceed that of Classes I and II combined by the observed amount or more. The 0.01 significance level indicates that were there really no differences in the rate of price change between the classes, the probability is only one chance in a hundred that the rate of price change in Classes I and II would exceed that in Classes III and IV by the observed amounts or more. Since 0.04 and 0.01 are low probabilities one can conclude that the differences in productivity and price change between the classes are real rather than the result of random variation.

7. Testing the differences between Class IV and the average of Classes I and II combined yields t values of 2.38 for growth in productivity and 3.11 for price change, using pooled variance estimates. The one-tailed significance levels of these differences are 0.01 for productivity growth and 0.002 for price change. The interpretation of these significance levels is exactly analogous to the interpretation in the preceding note.

8. For the difference in productivity growth the t value was 2.72 (0.01 significance level), while for the difference in price change the t value was 1.45 (0.10 significance level). These are one-tailed significance levels using pooled variance estimates.

9. The difference of 1.69 percent a year in the rate of growth in productivity has a t value of 3.84, while the difference of 0.92 percent in price change has a t value of 2.47. Both of these were computed using pooled variance estimates, and both have one-tailed significance levels beyond 0.01.

10. For productivity the t values were 3.46 (significant beyond 0.001) for 1947–1972 and 3.31 (significant at 0.002) for 1954–1972. For price change the t values were 1.67 (significant at 0.06) for 1947–1972 and 1.47 (significant at 0.08). These are one-tailed significance levels. They were computed using separate variance estimates because the F tests of the variances were too large to accept the hypothesis of equal variance.

11. Peltzman, in "Gains and Losses," p. 6, makes a similar point.

12. Steven Lustgarten, "Gains and Losses from Industrial Concentration: Comment," *Journal of Law and Economics*, vol. 22 (April 1979), pp. 183–90.

5
Summary and Conclusions

The data in tables 2 through 4 have shown that changes in concentration are related to changes in productivity and price levels. Specifically, increases in productivity are greater and price increases equal or smaller where concentration is increasing than where it is decreasing. The difference between industries is greater where the growth in output of an industry is above the median. For the period 1947–1972, among industries with growth rates above the median, the difference in the average rate of total factor growth in productivity between industries in which concentration ratios were increasing and those in which they were decreasing was more than one percentage point a year—a 50 percent higher rate of rise in productivity (see table 4). The difference in the average rate of price increase between these groups was almost half a percentage point a year—a 25 percent lower rate of price rise in industries in which concentration was increasing (table 4).

The gap between the rates of change in prices and productivity is important. In the absence of any increases in wage rates or profit rates, output prices could be expected to decrease at the same rate that total factor productivity increases. The fact that differences in productivity were greater than differences in prices suggests that increased concentration has led to greater compensation for either labor or capital or both. It is possible, then, that increased concentration has led to greater profits for producers, which, if true, appears to support the monopoly theory of concentration. One is forced to conclude, however, that if profits are greater, it is because costs are lower, not because prices are higher. Although producers (workers or owners of capital) may have been made better off by increasing concentration, it was also to the benefit—not the detriment—of consumers, who paid lower prices as a result because the major portion of the gains in productivity was passed on in lower prices.

Perhaps higher profits should be seen as the reward to producers for implementing cost-saving innovations. In a perfectly competitive environment with a zero cost of information and where all innovations are immediately imitated by all firms in an industry with no increased profits to the innovator, there would be little incentive to innovate. Consequently, innovations would be few. The higher profits earned by industries in which productivity has increased are an important incentive to continued growth in productivity.

The data examined in this study have important implications for public policy toward firms in concentrated industries and toward increases in concentration. Since increases in productivity are greater and price increases are smaller where concentration has increased, public policy that attempts to constrain the growth of large firms or to force divestiture will very likely prove harmful to consumers.

Appendix A

Mathematical Formulation of Productivity Function

Measuring Growth in Productivity

Let the production function for the ith firm in an industry be of the form:

$$q_{it} = z_{it} k_t^a \, l_t^b \tag{1}$$

where q, l, and k are output, labor, and capital respectively; a and b, the distribution parameters, z the efficiency parameter, and t time. Equation 1 implies that all firms in an industry use the same inputs but have different levels of output because of differences in z.

Growth in productivity can be measured as the ratio of the growth of *industry* output to the geometric weighted average growth of industry inputs:

$$\bar{Q}/\bar{K}^x \, \bar{L}^y \tag{2}$$

where upper-case letters denote industry aggregates, the "bar" refers to the ratio of current to base year values (for example, $\bar{Q} = Q_1/Q_0$) and weights x and y are the shares paid to capital and labor ($x + y = 1$). If (2) is applied to an industry of n firms ($K = nk$, $L = nl$, and $\bar{Z} = \Sigma_{i} z_{it}$), whose production functions are represented by (1), then the measure of productivity is:

$$\frac{\bar{Z} \, \bar{k}^a \, \bar{l}^b}{(n \, \bar{k})^x \, (nl)^y} = \frac{\bar{Z} \, \bar{K}^{a-x} \, \bar{L}^{b-y}}{\bar{n}^{a+b}} = z' \, \bar{K}^{a-x} \, \bar{L}^{b-y} \, \bar{n}^{1-a-b} \tag{3}$$

if we let $z' = \bar{Z}/\bar{n}$. Equation 3 is a fraction with the numerator equal to actual output growth and a denominator equal to hypothetical output growth under constant returns of scale and no change in the efficiency

33

parameters. The fraction could be greater than one attributable to (i) innovation among existing firms or exits of less efficient firms such that $z' > 1$, or (ii) industry growth ($\bar{K} > 1$ and $\bar{L} > 1$) coupled with economies of scale ($a \geqslant x$, $b \geqslant y$, and $a + b \geqslant 1$). A positive cross-section correlation between (3) and concentration can be interpreted as evidence that one or more of these alternatives is more important in concentrated than in atomistic industries.

Several measures of productivity are computed for each manufacturing industry. Conceptually, the most desirable is the measure of total factor productivity analogous to (2)

$$\bar{Q}/\bar{L}_p^{w1} \cdot \bar{L}_n^{w2} \cdot \bar{K}^{w3} \cdot \bar{X}^{w4}$$

where L_p, L_n, K, and X are production labor, nonproduction labor, capital, and all other inputs; while w_1 through w_4 are their respective factor shares of value added. The variable $\bar{Q}$ is the benchmark index of change in real output, L_p is industry aggregate production worker hours, and L_n is industry aggregate number of nonproduction workers. The values of L_p, L_n, w_1, and w_2 were taken directly from the Census of Manufactures. The values of K for 1948–1958 come from Kendrick (1973) and for 1958–1972 from Kendrick (1976). The values for 1947–1948 were obtained by extrapolating the trend for 1948–1954 for each industry. The same values of K (which are for two-digit industries in constant dollars) were assigned to each of the four-digit industries comprising a two-digit industry. The value of w_3 is the residual after subtracting the other factor shares. The value of X was computed on the basis of the difference between industry value added as defined by the Census of Manufactures and industry value added as defined in the *Input-Output Study for the U.S.* The latter follows the national income definition and excludes from value added those services purchased from other businesses such as advertising, communications, maintenance and repair, rents and royalties. The difference between these two measures of value added represents production inputs that are not counted in L_p or L_n or K and are thus designated "all other inputs." Since the input-output data were not available on a four-digit basis for every census year, the dollar values of X were estimated by letting the difference between the census and input-output definitions for 1963 remain a constant percentage of the census value added in earlier and later census years. This gives w_4. The values of $\bar{X}$ were computed by deflating the ratio of current and base year dollar values of X by a price index for services (with the index set at 100 for the base year). The deflator used was the consumer price index for services, less rent.

Because of obvious difficulties in computing reliable measures of K and X, a labor productivity measure was also computed:

$$\bar{Q} / \bar{L}_p^{s1} \cdot \bar{L}_n^{s2}$$

where s_1 and s_2 represent the shares of payroll attributable to production and nonproduction labor.

A third variable analyzed is the industry price change:

$$\overline{VA}/\bar{Q}$$

where VA is value added.

Statistical Caveats

Changes in real value added per unit of total factor input or per unit of labor are not perfect measures of changes in productivity (average value of output per unit of input) for several reasons. Insofar as firms may change the reporting location of some workers or of some equipment such as computers and accounting machinery from establishments whose data are compiled by the Bureau of the Census to central headquarters or vice versa, increase in value added per unit of input may be over- or understated. Also, insofar as price indexes are not fully adjusted for changes in the quality of product, changes in real value added may be under- or overestimated (the former being more likely than the latter in an economy with rising per capita income).

A relative rise or fall in the prices of materials used in an industry and the concomitant rise or fall in product price may cause a progressively larger or smaller deflation of value added and a spurious appearance of relative decline or rise in productivity. In addition, the use of changes in capital stock in the two-digit industry of which a four-digit industry is a component, as a surrogate for the change in the four-digit industry's capital stock, will introduce some inaccuracies in the measure of changes in total factor productivity. Also, the substitution of outside providers of services such as advertising agencies, manufacturers' agents, building and machinery maintenance services, or the purchase of patent rights on a royalty basis for employees such as salesmen, custodians, and research and development personnel, or vice versa, can affect value-added measures per unit of input without real changes in productivity.

Insofar as these various biases are not correlated with concentration or with changes in concentration, they will blur the relation-

FIGURE 1

PRODUCTIVITY GROWTH AND CONCENTRATION CHANGE FOR
HIGH-GROWTH INDUSTRIES, 1954–1972

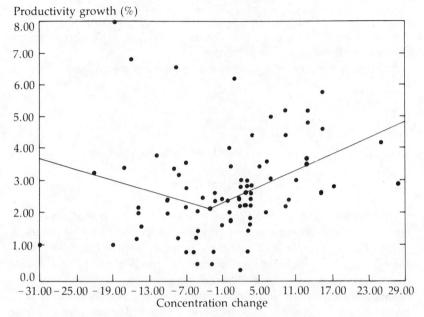

Productivity growth (%)

Concentration change

ships measured in this study but should not seriously affect the major conclusions.

Regression Equations

In figures 1 and 2, the data underlying table 4 are plotted for the high-growth industries for 1954–1972. In both figures concentration change is measured on the horizontal axis. In figure 1 productivity growth is measured on the vertical axis, and in figure 2 price change is on the vertical axis. Inspection of the plots shows that the relation between concentration and productivity growth can be described as having a "V" shape. There is evidence, as suggested in table 4, that large decreases as well as large increases in concentration result in higher productivity. The plots also suggest, however, that zero concentration change is not the point where productivity growth is lowest. That is, industries with moderate declines in concentration have lower productivity than industries with no change in concentration. In order to determine the point of lowest productivity growth, a least-squares

FIGURE 2

PRICE CHANGE AND CONCENTRATION CHANGE FOR
HIGH-GROWTH INDUSTRIES, 1954–1972

Price change (%)

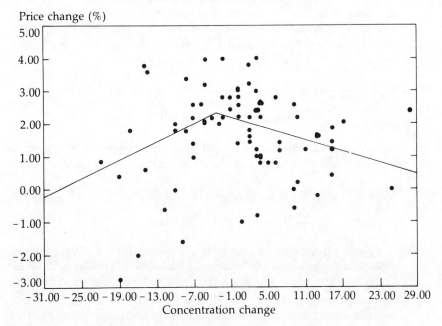

Concentration change

regression of the following form was fitted to the data:

$$Y_a = a_1 + a_2 D_1 (X - X^*) + a_3 D_2 (X - X^*) \qquad (4)$$

where

D_1 = 1 if $X \geqslant X^*$ and D_1 = 0 otherwise

D_2 = if $X < X^*$ and D_2 = 0 otherwise

Y_a = rate of total factor productivity growth

X = change in concentration

X^* = concentration change where productivity growth is lowest

This specification divides the domain of concentration change at X^* and estimates a slope for each segment with a common intercept at X^*. The correct value of X^* was determined by estimating the regression in equation 4 using alternative values of X^* ranging from –10 to + 10. The value of X^* yielding the highest R^2 statistic (that is, explaining the

37

largest portion of the total variation of productivity growth and concentration change) was chosen as the correct X^*. The R^2 statistics for equation 4 estimated for alternative values of X^* are shown in table 5. The behavior of R^2 over the range of values of X^* follows a pattern of continuous increases followed by continuous decreases with the maximum value at $X^* = -3$. With $X^* = -3$, the resulting regression equation is:

$$Y_a = 2.10 + 0.085\, D_1(X - X^*) - 0.056\, D_2(X - X^*) \qquad R^2 = 0.119$$

$$\qquad\quad (3.23) \qquad\qquad\qquad (1.69) \qquad\qquad N = 81$$

The t-statistics are shown in parentheses. Estimating the same equation with price change (Y_b) as the dependent variable yields:

$$Y_b = 2.23 - 0.053\, D_1(X - X^*) + 0.090\, D_2(X - X^*) \qquad R^2 = 0.109$$

$$\qquad\quad (2.23) \qquad\qquad\qquad (3.01) \qquad\qquad N = 81$$

These equations confirm the expected "V" shape of the productivity-concentration relation and show a corresponding inverted "V" shape of the price-change-concentration relation. The graphs of these equations are shown in figures 1 and 2. For concentration changes above -3, the regression indicates that the rate of

---

TABLE 5

R^2 STATISTICS FOR ALTERNATIVE VALUES OF X^* (TOTAL FACTOR PRODUCTIVITY GROWTH AS DEPENDENT VARIABLE)

X^*	R^2	X^*	R^2
−10	.067	10	.041
−9	.074	9	.044
−8	.086	8	.050
−7	.097	7	.057
−6	.108	6	.065
−5	.117	5	.073
−4	.118	4	.082
−3	.119	3	.090
−2	.115	2	.095
−1	.110	1	.097
0	.103		

SOURCE: Appendix B.

productivity growth is greater by 0.81 percent per year, and the rate of price increase is lower by 0.53 percent per year, for each 10-point increase in the concentration ratio. For concentration changes below –3 the rate of productivity growth is higher by 0.56 percent per year and the rate price increase lower by 0.90 percent per year for each 10 point decrease in concentration. These results are quite stable for values of X^* in the neighborhood of –3. At $X^* = 0$ for example, which is the value implied in Peltzman's study, the estimates of the slope coefficients in the productivity equation were 0.89 ($t = 2.98$) and –0.039 ($t = 1.12$) for increasing and decreasing concentration respectively. In the corresponding price change equation the slopes were –0.061 ($t = 2.26$) and 0.67 ($t = 2.74$).

The magnitude of the regression coefficients suggests that for increases in concentration the price-reducing impact falls short of the productivity-raising impact, but for decreases in concentration the price-reducing impact exceeds the productivity-raising impact. The difference in the effect on productivity and price is evidence that profit rates, or wage and salary rates, or both rose when concentration increased and fell when it decreased. This is consistent with the theory that where firms are few in number competition will be lessened, thus leading to higher profits. It therefore provides partial support for the monopoly theory. The evidence does not signify, however, that deconcentration will benefit consumers. It signifies only that while consumers would be faced with higher prices as a result of deconcentration, the magnitude of the price rises would not be as high as the productivity loss because part of the inefficiency created by deconcentration would be absorbed by the firm's stockholders or employees.

Appendix B

TABLE B-1

CHANGE IN PRODUCTIVITY, INDUSTRY CONCENTRATION, AND PRICE LEVELS, 1947–1972, 1954–1972

Data Used in Constructing Tables 2–4

Standard Industrial Classification Code	1947–1972				1954–1972			
	Percent annual change in total factor productivity	Percent annual change in labor productivity	Change in concentration	Percent annual change in price levels	Percent annual change in total factor productivity	Percent annual change in labor productivity	Change in concentration	Percent annual change in price levels
2011	—	—	—	—	3.17	4.370	–17.0	1.915
2021	—	—	—	—	4.39	7.282	29.0	–0.669
2024	—	—	—	—	1.94	3.858	– 7.0	1.090
2034	4.471	3.160	–23.0	2.517	1.92	1.078	–15.0	3.828
2041	—	—	—	—	1.60	3.798	– 7.0	1.929
2043	1.394	2.586	11.0	3.689	2.23	3.781	2.0	3.259
2044	3.784	4.617	10.0	0.515	3.02	4.709	2.0	2.166
2046	2.483	3.167	–14.0	0.935	3.87	4.593	–12.0	–0.654
2051	1.052	1.894	13.0	3.656	1.73	2.800	9.0	2.921
2063	3.183	4.342	–2.0	0.602	3.49	4.350	0.0	1.373

2065	2.590	3.426	15.0	1.377	3.34	4.295	13.0	1.563
2066	0.915	1.552	6.0	2.734	1.60	2.010	4.0	4.002
2067	1.150	2.079	17.0	2.720	0.75	0.385	1.0	3.254
2074	2.944	4.974	0.0	−1.399	1.17	3.576	−4.0	0.562
2075	6.414	5.940	10.0	−2.352	4.82	4.978	13.0	−0.109
2082	3.076	4.733	31.0	1.102	4.14	5.697	25.0	0.095
2084	3.649	3.763	27.0	0.943	5.83	3.879	15.0	0.474
2085	2.800	4.507	−28.0	0.661	3.41	5.302	−17.0	1.749
2086	2.309	2.412	4.0	2.768	2.79	2.790	4.0	2.593
2087	4.947	6.649	16.0	0.900	5.22	6.125	13.0	1.674
2097	−1.843	1.292	10.0	3.357	−1.34	1.173	6.0	3.820
2098	1.906	2.582	15.0	2.769	1.93	2.440	12.0	3.015
2111	1.366	1.241	−6.0	4.723	1.95	1.638	2.0	3.678
2121	2.858	5.145	15.0	1.028	2.79	5.375	12.0	1.000
2131	−0.911	2.377	10.0	4.974	−1.72	1.253	13.0	4.583
2141	0.962	2.343	−21.0	3.724	0.34	1.501	−12.0	4.531
2211	—	—	—	—	2.69	3.161	13.0	1.805
2221	6.263	5.852	8.0	−2.238	5.17	5.237	9.0	−0.055
2241	—	—	—	—	2.51	2.585	7.0	1.617
2253	2.273	1.505	8.0	2.270	2.42	1.756	10.0	2.228
2254	1.873	2.813	25.0	1.755	2.68	3.375	20.0	2.668
2284	—	—	—	—	1.85	2.452	−4.0	2.834
2291	1.598	1.621	−5.0	2.547	2.38	2.557	10.0	1.719
2292	0.348	1.556	8.0	1.027	0.87	1.859	11.0	1.899
2293	2.610	2.613	−13.0	1.266	3.57	3.688	−4.0	0.475
2294	2.390	3.064	31.0	2.081	2.90	3.723	36.0	1.434

(Table continues)

41

TABLE B–1 (continued)

Standard Industrial Classification Code	1947–1972				1954–1972			
	Percent annual change in total factor productivity	Percent annual change in labor productivity	Change in concentration	Percent annual change in price levels	Percent annual change in total factor productivity	Percent annual change in labor productivity	Change in concentration	Percent annual change in price levels
2295	2.416	2.314	1.0	2.614	3.24	2.820	−8.0	1.745
2298	1.761	2.599	3.0	0.762	1.88	2.361	−4.0	0.616
2311	1.310	1.164	10.0	2.540	1.16	1.516	8.0	3.261
2321	3.095	2.536	3.0	1.548	1.88	2.628	5.0	2.480
2322	3.478	2.323	2.0	1.930	2.02	2.052	6.0	2.757
2323	1.305	0.822	6.0	2.994	0.57	1.012	10.0	3.529
2327	3.295	2.225	17.0	1.394	2.75	2.685	17.0	1.983
2331	—	—	—	—	3.02	3.109	7.0	1.295
2337	—	—	—	—	−0.35	0.865	10.0	2.761
2341	2.640	1.717	9.0	1.543	0.77	1.457	7.0	2.866
2342	2.207	2.249	15.0	1.969	1.28	2.398	5.0	1.727
2351	2.000	2.544	10.0	0.849	2.02	3.290	10.0	1.085
2363	—	—	—	—	0.01	1.356	4.0	2.340
2384	2.111	1.685	14.0	1.513	0.15	1.120	9.0	3.019
2385	3.645	2.886	8.0	1.459	3.01	3.566	11.0	1.193
2386	2.761	1.681	−5.0	2.558	0.79	1.325	1.0	4.189
2387	2.795	2.826	−2.0	1.891	2.45	3.369	2.0	2.023
2391	3.797	2.556	17.0	0.499	2.68	2.394	15.0	1.337

2392	3.054	2.720	-10.0	1.318	2.77	2.938	2.0	1.393
2393	0.002	-0.908	-26.0	3.664	0.34	-0.528	-18.0	4.830
2394	3.562	3.123	13.0	0.921	2.58	3.414	9.0	0.864
2397	3.527	3.127	2.0	0.485	2.11	3.010	4.0	1.251
2491	0.972	1.883	5.0	2.080	1.43	2.402	6.0	3.018
2514	2.467	2.251	-13.0	1.858	1.83	2.210	-3.0	1.835
2519	—	—	—	—	0.96	2.419	-31.0	2.354
2521	1.422	1.448	4.0	3.342	1.94	1.869	0.0	2.925
2522	2.292	1.911	-8.0	2.802	2.45	2.197	-4.0	2.215
2531	—	—	—	—	2.38	2.469	-10.0	1.813
2642	1.686	2.129	1.0	2.489	2.23	2.524	4.0	2.215
2646	3.242	2.679	-11.0	1.606	2.88	2.347	3.0	1.148
2711	1.497	1.905	-4.0	2.710	1.50	2.247	-1.0	2.750
2721	1.895	2.884	-8.0	2.142	0.74	1.680	-3.0	3.201
2731	1.117	2.703	1.0	4.071	0.89	2.075	-2.0	3.964
2732	—	—	—	—	2.24	2.352	3.0	2.345
2741	3.184	2.844	7.0	2.467	2.53	2.575	-2.0	2.728
2753	2.203	2.825	-10.0	2.562	2.43	3.140	4.0	2.531
2771	2.950	3.853	31.0	2.403	2.94	4.294	28.0	2.340
2791	1.852	1.841	-3.0	2.829	1.86	2.043	0.0	2.866
2793	0.705	1.705	5.0	2.654	0.95	2.201	7.0	2.705
2794	-0.307	1.334	19.0	2.865	-0.86	1.225	20.0	2.917
2812	3.077	6.385	2.0	1.151	3.00	6.802	3.0	-0.848
2813	5.975	9.336	-18.0	-1.175	8.04	11.566	-19.0	-2.836
2816	—	—	—	—	1.17	3.213	-15.0	0.267
2822	2.474	4.253	—	0.577	4.36	5.687	9.0	-0.537

(Table continues)

43

TABLE B–1 (continued)

Standard Industrial Classification Code	1947–1972				1954–1972			
	Percent annual change in total factor productivity	Percent annual change in labor productivity	Change in concentration	Percent annual change in price levels	Percent annual change in total factor productivity	Percent annual change in labor productivity	Change in concentration	Percent annual change in price levels
2831	5.925	5.667	−1.0	−0.848	6.67	5.768	−9.0	−1.568
2834	5.968	7.756	−2.0	−0.954	6.13	7.592	1.0	−0.999
2844	3.284	5.954	14.0	1.962	3.52	5.273	13.0	1.653
2851	0.448	2.087	−5.0	2.383	1.31	2.679	−5.0	1.912
2869	—	—	—	—	6.76	7.910	−16.0	−1.988
2875	—	—	—	—	0.70	3.107	4.0	2.878
2892	—	—	—	—	0.54	2.065	−12.0	2.489
2893	1.325	2.415	−18.0	1.604	2.16	3.091	−15.0	0.674
2895	0.317	3.337	−4.0	1.454	1.77	4.758	4.0	0.705
2951	4.514	3.065	−4.0	2.213	3.91	2.176	0.0	2.594
2952	1.692	2.601	6.0	2.303	2.14	3.076	9.0	2.523
2992	—	—	—	—	2.20	3.743	3.0	2.992
2999	—	—	—	—	2.10	5.959	16.0	2.525
3031	2.422	4.703	−6.0	1.051	−0.07	4.106	5.0	0.576
3111	0.773	1.664	−10.0	0.788	1.26	2.162	−1.0	2.459
3131	−1.830	−0.203	−13.0	4.035	−1.72	0.120	−5.0	4.574
3142	—	—	—	—	0.66	1.130	20.0	3.359
3171	1.641	1.646	7.0	2.223	0.68	0.914	6.0	3.555

3211	—	—	—	—	2.42	4.419	2.0	1.820
3221	0.410	1.206	-8.0	4.156	1.13	1.707	-8.0	3.364
3229	2.483	3.776	15.0	2.800	2.33	3.551	-1.0	2.338
3241	1.362	3.873	-4.0	3.233	1.07	4.079	-5.0	1.971
3251	1.123	2.582	7.0	2.719	0.76	2.507	4.0	2.485
3255	-0.065	1.760	8.0	3.910	0.88	2.529	6.0	3.149
3261	1.864	2.988	0.0	2.000	2.15	3.561	-7.0	1.386
3262	-0.763	-0.419	19.0	3.177	1.42	2.422	20.0	2.817
3263	-0.993	-0.860	27.0	4.275	-1.00	-0.956	28.0	4.337
3264	1.170	1.866	2.0	2.589	2.37	2.807	0.0	2.249
3274	0.966	3.147	7.0	2.699	1.45	4.013	2.0	2.340
3275	2.550	3.498	-5.0	1.241	2.05	3.728	-10.0	-0.036
3281	—	—	—	—	2.57	4.200	6.0	0.565
3291	0.810	1.811	0.0	3.255	1.18	2.297	-1.0	2.635
3312	—	—	—	—	1.59	2.482	-10.0	2.210
3313	—	—	—	—	2.22	3.462	-3.0	1.198
3321	1.324	2.173	18.0	3.301	2.18	2.481	8.0	2.565
3322	1.645	2.231	17.0	3.026	1.18	1.504	2.0	3.644
3333	1.817	3.663	13.0	0.782	1.79	3.411	10.0	1.113
3411	1.443	2.236	-12.0	4.536	1.61	2.254	-14.0	3.609
3421	2.214	3.790	14.0	2.373	2.14	3.557	6.0	2.489
3425	0.672	1.990	-15.0	3.198	1.77	2.775	-5.0	2.407
3444	1.925	2.188	-12.0	2.652	2.38	2.488	-10.0	2.005
3451	1.745	2.257	-11.0	2.339	2.05	2.595	-5.0	1.967
3462	0.641	1.682	5.0	3.501	1.44	2.473	2.0	2.867
3471	0.793	0.814	-10.0	3.519	1.30	1.356	-5.0	3.227

(Table continues)

45

TABLE B-1 (continued)

Standard Industrial Classification Code	1947–1972				1954–1972			
	Percent annual change in total factor productivity	Percent annual change in labor productivity	Change in concentration	Percent annual change in price levels	Percent annual change in total factor productivity	Percent annual change in labor productivity	Change in concentration	Percent annual change in price levels
3494	0.932	1.631	-13.0	3.594	1.19	1.558	-6.0	3.163
3537	1.088	1.621	-7.0	3.465	1.80	2.288	0.0	3.001
3541	0.614	1.297	2.0	3.621	0.04	0.857	3.0	2.587
3551	0.054	1.355	0.0	3.933	0.28	1.453	2.0	3.520
3552	0.913	1.976	1.0	2.564	2.15	2.964	-1.0	1.994
3553	—	—	—	—	2.60	3.831	3.0	1.023
3554	0.766	1.446	4.0	3.497	0.52	1.009	-2.0	3.161
3555	0.321	1.634	11.0	3.794	1.60	2.622	4.0	2.555
3562	3.082	4.221	-9.0	1.027	3.54	4.566	-7.0	1.057
3564	1.083	1.886	-13.0	3.235	0.74	1.496	-5.0	3.138
3582	0.809	2.601	-6.0	2.084	2.08	3.526	2.0	0.735
3612	1.562	3.110	-14.0	1.480	0.92	2.520	-19.0	0.496
3621	0.652	3.055	-12.0	2.136	0.79	3.293	-3.0	1.206
3623	0.246	1.233	-5.0	2.846	0.15	1.023	2.0	3.790
3624	1.103	2.914	-7.0	2.447	0.83	2.586	-6.0	2.626
3633	2.498	5.307	43.0	1.561	2.67	5.334	15.0	1.784
3636	0.725	3.286	7.0	3.643	2.10	4.631	3.0	3.739
3641	0.370	3.127	-2.0	2.920	0.30	2.802	-3.0	1.909
3652	3.458	4.347	-31.0	-0.468	3.30	3.204	-22.0	0.765

3691	-0.084	2.760	-5.0	2.122	0.74	2.915	-7.0	2.546
3693	-0.379	1.376	-4.0	5.113	0.74	2.123	3.0	4.063
3694	1.391	3.349	-2.0	2.690	1.39	3.479	3.0	2.455
3731	2.977	3.411	4.0	1.367	2.54	2.789	4.0	1.029
3732	2.900	3.361	-17.0	1.943	2.73	2.926	-7.0	2.190
3751	3.455	4.645	23.0	0.967	4.56	5.137	15.0	1.219
3843	-0.201	1.996	-5.0	3.903	0.47	1.985	-5.0	3.901
3851	1.492	3.472	-2.0	2.103	2.41	3.931	2.0	1.534
3861	3.732	6.352	13.0	2.268	4.29	6.719	a	1.719
3942	2.699	3.250	-17.0	0.594	2.51	3.219	3.0	0.870
3949	4.234	4.493	4.0	1.226	5.09	4.167	7.0	1.319
3955	2.928	3.680	5.0	1.025	3.55	3.871	6.0	0.820
3961	2.022	3.460	-7.0	1.172	2.67	3.742	3.0	1.494
3962	2.777	3.908	23.0	1.044	3.93	5.159	24.0	0.605
3963	1.980	4.054	11.0	1.290	1.82	3.708	11.0	1.944
3964	3.903	5.538	9.0	0.026	4.41	5.507	4.0	0.938
3991	-0.055	1.478	2.0	2.825	1.90	2.611	3.0	1.870
3993	2.430	2.769	1.0	2.164	2.40	2.690	-2.0	2.169
3995	2.334	3.916	-1.0	1.374	3.48	4.428	5.0	0.884
3996	0.233	3.393	11.0	2.722	2.35	5.088	4.0	1.787

NOTE: Dashes indicate 1947 data were not available or were not comparable to later data.

a. 1954 concentration ratio is not comparable to 1972.

SOURCE: U.S. Bureau of the Census, *Census of Manufactures 1947, 1954, 1958, 1963, 1967, 1972.*

TABLE B–2

RATIO OF THE NUMBER OF FIRMS IN 1972 TO THE NUMBER OF FIRMS IN 1947 AND 1954 IN SELECTED U.S. INDUSTRIES

Standard Industrial Classification Code	Description	Ratio of Firms 1972 to Firms 1947	Ratio of Firms 1972 to Firms 1954
2011	Meat slaughtering plants	1.147	1.029
2021	Creamery butter	n.a.	0.172
2024	Ice cream and frozen dessert	n.a.	0.408
2034	Dehydrated foods products	1.108	1.118
2041	Flour mills	0.314	0.491
2043	Cereal preparations	0.618	0.919
2044	Rice milling	0.640	0.738
2046	Wet corn milling	0.553	0.481
2051	Bread and related products	0.468	0.512
2063	Beet sugar	0.941	1.067
2065	Confectionery products	0.566	0.661
2066	Chocolate and cocoa products	1.258	1.444
2067	Chewing gum	0.429	0.556
2074	Cottonseed oil mills	0.418	0.510
2075	Soybean oil mills	0.514	0.982
2082	Malt liquors	0.267	0.411
2084	Wines and brandy	0.483	0.750
2085	Distilled liquor, except brandy	0.528	0.776
2086	Bottled and canned soft drinks	0.439	0.524
2087	Flavorings	0.601	0.660
2097	Manufactured ice	0.277	0.427
2098	Macaroni and spaghetti	0.817	0.792
2111	Cigarettes	0.684	1.083
2121	Cigars	0.140	0.285
2131	Chewing and smoking tobacco	0.431	0.483
2141	Tobacco stemming and redrying	0.495	0.639
2211	Weaving mills, cotton	n.a.	0.460
2221	Weaving mills, synthetics	0.593	0.646
2241	Narrow fabric mills	n.a.	0.663
2253	Knit outerwear mills	0.737	0.816
2254	Knit underwear mills	0.529	0.529
2284	Thread mills	n.a.	0.726
2291	Felt goods, not elsewhere classified	1.027	0.585

TABLE B–2 (continued)

Standard Industrial Classification Code	Description	Ratio of Firms 1972 to Firms 1947	Ratio of Firms 1972 to Firms 1954
2292	Lace goods	1.065	0.744
2293	Padding and upholstery filling	0.960	0.665
2294	Processed textile waste	0.576	0.515
2295	Coated fabric, not rubberized	1.745	1.796
2298	Cordage and twine	1.015	1.126
2311	Men's and boys' suits and coats	0.409	0.575
2321	Men's dress shirts and nightwear	0.562	0.618
2322	Men's and boys' underwear	0.713	0.931
2323	Men's and boys' neckwear	0.713	0.722
2327	Separate trousers	0.484	0.603
2331	Blouses	n.a.	0.719
2337	Women's suits, coats and skirts	n.a.	0.487
2341	Women's and children's underwear	0.414	0.476
2342	Corsets and allied garments	0.446	0.519
2351	Millinery	0.232	0.249
2363	Children's coats and suits	n.a.	0.387
2384	Robes and dressing gowns	0.465	0.534
2385	Waterproof outergarments	0.963	0.811
2386	Leather and sheeplined clothing	1.480	1.209
2387	Apparel belts	0.749	0.583
2391	Curtains and draperies	4.061	2.208
2392	House furnishings, not elsewhere classified	0.876	0.880
2393	Textile bags	0.949	0.800
2394	Canvas products	0.951	0.768
2397	Machine embroideries	0.823	0.742
2491	Wood preserving	2.272	1.644
2514	Metal household furniture	1.397	0.671
2519	Household furniture, not elsewhere classified	n.a.	2.275
2521	Wood office furniture	2.035	2.090
2522	Metal office furniture	1.660	1.361
2531	Public building furniture	n.a.	1.392

(Table continues)

TABLE B–2 (continued)

Standard Industrial Classification Code	Description	Ratio of Firms 1972 to Firms 1947	Ratio of Firms 1972 to Firms 1954
2642	Envelopes	1.254	1.047
2646	Pressed and molded pulp goods	1.684	1.230
2711	Newspapers	0.919	0.884
2721	Periodicals	1.164	1.218
2731	Books, publishing and printing	1.764	1.393
2732	Book printing	n.a.	1.139
2741	Miscellaneous publishing	3.452	2.182
2753	Engraving and plate printing	1.316	0.959
2771	Greeting card manufacturing	1.155	0.664
2791	Typesetting	2.346	1.725
2793	Photoengraving	0.773	0.660
2794	Electrotyping and stereotyping	0.351	0.329
2812	Alkalies and chlorine	1.556	1.647
2813	Industrial gases	1.522	1.040
2816	Inorganic pigments	n.a.	1.055
2822	Synthetic rubber	n.a.	3.846
2831	Biological products	2.000	1.837
2834	Pharmaceutical preparations	0.606	0.603
2844	Toilet preparations	0.857	0.856
2851	Paints and allied products	1.142	0.986
2869	Industrial organic chemicals, not elsewhere classified	n.a.	1.738
2875	Fertilizers, mixing only	1.172	1.011
2892	Explosives	n.a.	1.375
2893	Printing ink	1.411	1.133
2895	Carbon black	0.846	0.917
2951	Paving mixtures and blocks	3.214	2.321
2952	Asphalt felts and coatings	1.115	1.074
2992	Lubricating oils and greases	1.883	1.457
2999	Petroleum and coal products, not elsewhere classified	n.a.	1.077
3031	Reclaimed rubber	1.357	1.267
3111	Leather tanning and finishing	0.936	0.891
3131	Footwear cut stock	0.414	0.431

TABLE B–2 (continued)

Standard Industrial Classification Code	Description	Ratio of Firms 1972 to Firms 1947	Ratio of Firms 1972 to Firms 1954
3142	House slippers	n.a.	0.488
3171	Handbags and purses	0.594	0.607
3211	Flat glass	n.a.	0.688
3221	Glass containers	0.659	0.711
3229	Pressed and blown glass, not elsewhere classified	1.972	0.827
3241	Cement, hydraulic	1.027	1.119
3251	Brick and structural title	0.547	0.616
3255	Clay refractories	0.796	0.761
3261	Vitreous plumbing fixtures	1.615	1.680
3262	Vitreous china food utensils	1.231	1.000
3263	Fine earthenware food utensils	0.230	0.370
3264	Porcelain electrical supplies	1.574	1.762
3274	Lime	0.515	0.602
3275	Gypsum products	1.333	0.917
3281	Cut stone and stone products	n.a.	0.909
3291	Abrasive products	1.419	1.155
3312	Blast furnaces and steel mills	n.a.	n.a.
3313	Electrometallurgical products	2.700	1.588
3321	Gray iron foundries	0.575	0.676
3322	Malleable iron foundries	0.941	0.901
3333	Primary zinc	0.786	0.846
3411	Metal cans	1.314	1.229
3421	Cutlery	0.641	0.687
3425	Handsaws and saw blades	1.000	0.853
3444	Sheet metalwork	1.777	1.252
3451	Screw machine products	1.477	0.994
3462	Iron and steel forgings	1.050	1.020
3471	Plating and polishing	1.777	1.312
3494	Valves and pipe fittings	1.475	1.229
3537	Industrial trucks and tractors	1.901	1.551
3541	Metal-cutting machine tools	2.747	1.367
3551	Food products machinery	1.051	0.978
3552	Textile machinery	1.138	1.035
3553	Woodworking machinery	n.a.	0.927

(Table continues)

TABLE B–2 (continued)

Standard Industrial Classification Code	Description	Ratio of Firms 1972 to Firms 1947	Ratio of Firms 1972 to Firms 1954
3554	Paper industries machinery	1.410	1.245
3555	Printing trades machinery	1.743	1.529
3562	Ball and roller bearings	1.269	1.193
3564	Blowers and fans	1.925	1.731
3582	Commercial laundry equipment	0.840	0.990
3612	Transformers	1.254	1.105
3621	Motors and generators	1.451	1.222
3623	Electric welding apparatus	1.495	1.387
3624	Carbon and graphite products	1.611	1.349
3633	Household laundry equipment	0.339	0.417
3636	Sewing machines	1.043	0.923
3941	Electric lamps	2.943	2.943
3652	Phonograph records	5.594	3.978
3691	Storage batteries	0.673	0.566
3693	X-ray apparatus and tubes	0.833	0.736
3694	Engine electrical equipment	2.660	1.727
3731	Ship building and repairing	1.526	1.265
3732	Boat building and repairing	2.162	1.505
3751	Motorcycles, bicycles, and parts	2.920	4.977
3843	Dental equipment and supplies	1.842	1.995
3851	Ophthalmic goods	2.554	2.004
3861	Photographic equipment	1.604	1.297
3942	Dolls	0.634	0.490
3949	Sporting and athletic goods	1.709	1.431
3955	Carbon paper and inked ribbons	1.143	0.900
3961	Costume jewelry	0.894	0.680
3962	Artificial flowers	0.587	0.558
3963	Buttons	0.434	0.453
3964	Needles, pins, and fasteners	0.894	0.699
3991	Brooms and brushes	0.616	0.625
3993	Signs and advertising displays	1.666	1.239
3995	Umbrellas, parasols, and canes	0.903	0.876
3996	Hard-surface floor coverings	1.286	1.800

n.a. = data not available or not comparable between years.
SOURCE: U.S. Department of Commerce, Bureau of the Census, *Census of Manufactures*, 1972; *Concentration Ratios in Manufacturing*, MC 76 (SR)-2.

SELECTED AEI PUBLICATIONS